My Pet

My Pet Cats

by **LeeAnne Engfer**
photographs by **Andy King**

Lerner Publications Company • Minneapolis

To my parents, who got me started on cats—L.E.

Acknowledgments

The author and publisher would like to thank Joshua Borowicz, Julie Daniels, Stefan Daniels, and Zoë Daniels, who were photographed for this book. Thanks also to Jennifer Krohn; to the Animal Humane Society of Hennepin County, Golden Valley, Minnesota; and to PETsMART and VETsMART, St. Paul, Minnesota.

Photo on p. 14 by Nancy Smedstad. Photos on pp. 25, 33, & 42 by Jim Simondet.

Library of Congress Cataloging-in-Publication Data

Engfer, LeeAnne, 1963–
    My pet cats / by LeeAnne Engfer ; photographs by Andy King.
       p.   cm. — (All about pets)
    Includes bibliographical references and index.
    Summary: Text and photographs follow nine-year-old Zoë and her family as they adopt two kittens from an animal shelter and watch them grow up.
    ISBN 0-8225-2258-6 (hardcover)
    ISBN 0-8225-9793-4 (paperback)
    1. Cats—Juvenile literature. [1. Cats. 2. Pets.] I. King, Andy, ill. II. Title. III. Series
SF445.7.E54   1997
636.8—dc21   96–47304

Manufactured in the United States of America
1 2 3 4 5 6 — JR — 02 01 00 99 98 97

Contents

Kittens are the best birthday present!

These are my kittens soon after I got them. In this picture, they are only three months old.

My name is Zoë, and next week is my birthday. I'll be 10. Last year for my birthday, I got the best present ever—two cats. Well, they were kittens when I got them. But now they're over a year old. The kitties have the same birthday as me, March 10. I'm a Pisces—the fish. I *love* to swim. The kitties hate to swim! We tried to give them a bath, and they made a really funny noise. You know when water touches a hot pan, it goes *pfft...pop?* The cats sounded like steam coming off a pot. Then they popped out of the bathtub.

It's been great watching the kitties grow up. I learned fast how to take care of them. The hardest part was deciding what to name them!

Aunt Sarah tells stories about her cat, Luna. My mom and I don't always believe them.

I wanted a cat since I was little. But my dad wasn't sure he would like having a cat. He never had any pets before. My mom's family had cats and dogs when she was growing up, so she is used to animals.

One reason I love cats is because of Mica. Mica is a black kitty who belongs to my friend Sena. I like how Mica chases his tail and jumps up in my lap. He likes to have his belly rubbed. My aunt Sarah has a cat named Luna, who is gray with gold eyes. She is shy, but sweet. Sarah says that she doesn't own Luna—Luna owns her.

When my mom asked me what I wanted for my birthday last year, I told her, "A cat." She asked if I could take care of it myself. I would have to feed the cat and play with it and change the litter box. I knew I could do the chores. I also had to talk my dad into it, but finally he said okay. I asked my brother Stefan if he minded. He's 12. Even though he was jealous that I was the one getting the cat, he liked the idea.

Stefan and I get along pretty well. He was excited about getting a cat, too.

Dad wasn't sure he wanted a cat. Mom was easier to convince.

My parents said they would pay for the cost of keeping a cat. First you have to buy the kitten, unless you get it for free. You also have to buy supplies, like a litter box. Supplies cost about $50 to $100. Food costs $5 to $15 a month. Litter is about $5 to $10 a month.

To get your cat sterilized ("fixed" so it won't have babies) can cost $50 to $100. You also have to pay for shots and checkups at a vet. The vet can cost around $100 a year—more if your cat gets sick. So a cat is not the cheapest pet. On the other hand, it's not the most expensive either. (Just try asking your parents for a horse!)

I was worried that a cat would get lonely during the day. My mom and dad work full time, and I'm at school. Some people think cats like to be left alone. They don't need to be taken out for walks. You can leave them alone all day if you have to. But cats need company, just like people do. Aunt Sarah said that we should get two cats. That way they would have each other for company.

So we knew we wanted two cats. We still had a few other decisions to make. My mom and I talked about what kind of cats to get. We didn't need purebred cats. They are expensive, and plain house cats were fine with me anyway.

I read about cats before I got them. I watched a video about cats at the pet store, too.

Allergies to Cats

Some people are allergic to cats and dogs. They are not allergic to the animals themselves, but to their dander. Dander is dead skin that naturally flakes off. (It is too small to notice.) When people who have allergies are around cats, they sneeze and their eyes water. After a while they may have trouble breathing. It can be very uncomfortable.

There are things pet owners can do for visitors with allergies. It helps to keep the cats well groomed. You should comb or brush them often. You can also rub them down with a damp sponge. When a person with allergies visits, you can put the cats in a separate room or in the basement. (Make sure they have food, water, and their litter box.)

Pet stores sell liquids that you can rub on your cat's coat. These liquids are supposed to make it easier for people with allergies to be around cats. People who are allergic to pets can also take medicines or use nasal (nose) sprays. These may make them breathe more easily around animals and stop sneezing.

All of these things may help people who have allergies to cats. But they probably work for just short periods of time. In most cases, people who are allergic to cats or dogs just have to live without them. They can always choose fish as pets.

We talked about whether to get kittens or adult cats. I really wanted kittens. My mom called the veterinarian in our neighborhood for advice. She said we should try to find two littermates (kittens who were born together). They would be used to playing together. The kittens should be at least eight weeks old. If kittens are taken from their mother too early, they might get sick later or behave badly.

Getting pets is a family decision. We talked about it a lot.

Many cats get lost, and a lot of them never find their way home. They become strays.

We also had to decide where to get our kittens. Sena's cat, Mica, was a stray. He just showed up on her family's back porch one day. He looked skinny and didn't have a collar. Sena's family put up flyers in the neighborhood: "Cat Found!" But no one called. So they kept him, and now he's part of the family. I didn't find any stray cats, though.

We could have gone to the pet store, but instead we went to an animal shelter called the Humane Society. It takes in all kinds of animals that people don't want or can't keep anymore. If the animals are not adopted, they are put to death. It's so sad. That's why I wanted to get our kitties from the Humane Society. Anyway, kittens cost more at the pet store.

Before we went to the Humane Society, we got our house ready for the kittens. We went to a pet supply store and bought a bunch of stuff. We bought a litter box and litter, two ceramic food dishes, and plastic bowls for water. We also got a bag of kitten food and some kitty treats.

The store had hundreds of toys—catnip balls, toy mice, all kinds of things with feathers and fur. I wanted to buy something.

"No, Zoë," my mom said. "We're already spending a lot of money."

I was disappointed, but I knew she was right.

Now we were ready to go to the pet shelter to pick out our kittens!

The supply store was huge! Mom didn't want me to buy any toys yet, but I decided what I'd buy later.

Before we left for the shelter, we put the food and water dishes in the kitchen.

CHAPTER 2

How would I ever decide?

We went to the Humane Society in May, two months *after* my birthday. We had to wait until then because the Humane Society didn't have any kittens in March.

On the way to the shelter, I asked my mom what color cats she wanted. She said she liked any color. I love black and white cats, or gray ones, like my aunt's. But tabbies (striped cats) are nice, too. So are tortoiseshells, which are a mixture of black, orange, and creamy white. What if I couldn't decide? My mom said that if I couldn't make up my mind, we could come back another time.

At the Humane Society, we went straight to the room where they have the kittens and puppies. It smelled funny—kind of gross. There was a lot of barking and meowing. The room was crowded with people peering into cages or holding a kitten or puppy. I felt nervous. I wanted to make sure to choose healthy kittens.

I had checked out some cat books from the library, so I knew what to look for. Healthy kittens are lively and curious. They play, run, and wrestle with other kittens, and they are affectionate.

If a kitten is friendly and active, it's probably healthy.

One kitten came up to me like it was saying hello. The first two kittens I looked at weren't very playful, though.

I stopped at every cage and looked carefully at each kitten. They were all so cute! How would I ever decide? I liked one black and white kitten. But when I tried to pet her, she seemed scared. I saw some orange and white kittens in another cage. I stuck my hand in their cage. One of them came right up and rubbed its nose on my finger. I petted it and picked it up. It purred. "I like this one," I told my mom. We took that kitten and another orange kitten into a room down the hall. The shelter lets people use these rooms to spend time alone with the animals.

I was kind of scared to hold the kittens. I was afraid they'd scratch me, or I'd hurt them. The orange kittens were cute, but they didn't seem very lively.

After we came out, a shelter worker brought two new kittens to a cage. "Look," my mom said. "Aren't they sweet?"

They *were* sweet. One kitty, the female, was a dark tortoiseshell. The male was orange and white. My mom and I each picked up one of the kittens. We brought them into the room and set them down on the floor. They looked a little lost at first. Then one attacked the other and they started playing— two cute, clumsy balls of fur.

These kittens were already playmates.

A kitten's coat should be clean and shiny, with no signs of dandruff.

The vet had told us to check the kittens' eyes, ears, and noses. These kittens had clear eyes. Their ears looked clean. Their tiny noses were cool and dry. I ruffled their fur backward. Their coats seemed very clean, and they didn't scratch at themselves like they had fleas. I made my mom look at their rear ends to make sure they were clean, too.

"What do you think?" Mom asked.

"I think these are the ones," I said. I was already in love with them.

We took the kittens up to the counter. First we had to answer some questions on a form. The shelter tries to make sure that the pets are a good match for the families who adopt them. A woman who worked there looked over our answers and gave us the okay.

The Humane Society had already given the kittens their first shots, or vaccinations. Kittens usually are vaccinated for distemper, rabies, flu, and the feline leukemia virus. They get some shots before they are 12 weeks old. Our kittens were about 12 weeks old when we got them. In two or three months, we would have to take them to the vet for more shots. After that, they only need vaccinations once a year.

The Humane Society asks lots of questions. They want to be sure that the pets will have good homes.

The Humane Society charged $30 for each kitten. The price included the vaccinations. It also included a certificate that would pay for them to be sterilized later. We paid for the kittens—and this time my mom let me buy a few toys, too.

Finally we were ready to go home. We put the kitties into the plastic cat carrier we borrowed from Aunt Sarah. The whole way home they cried, a very sad little "mew mew." Most cats are afraid when they ride in a car. I felt kind of sad, too, about not choosing the other two kittens. "Don't worry," my mom said. "Someone will adopt them."

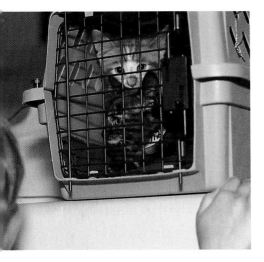

My kittens were coming home! I felt bad for the kittens I couldn't take with me.

The orange kitten was scared. When he hid behind the plant, he looked so tiny!

When we got to our house, we set the carrier on the floor in the kitchen. I opened the door. The tortoiseshell kitten came out first, very slowly. She began to explore the house. But the orange kitten was afraid to move. He just sat in the carrier and looked out. Finally he got brave. He crept out and walked around the kitchen. He jumped on a chair, and then he went into the dining room. He went into the corner behind a tall plant.

We put out food and water for them in the kitchen. The female found the litter box and used it right away.

That night, I went to bed very happy. I was hoping the kittens would sleep with me. But Mom said we should just let them sleep wherever they wanted. I woke up in the middle of the night and went downstairs to see the kittens. I couldn't find them at first. I searched everywhere. At last I found them in the bathroom. They were huddled together behind the door. I bent down to pet them, and the orange one hissed at me! It was such a tiny hiss—not at all fierce—that it made me laugh.

The kittens got used to the house in a few days.

Dangers to Cats

You've probably heard the old saying, "Curiosity killed the cat." Because kittens and cats are curious and playful, accidents can happen. Since cats don't really have nine lives, cat owners should try to prevent accidents. Here are some things you can do to keep your cat safe:

- Keep **dangerous household products** out of a cat's reach. Antifreeze, often used in cars, is especially deadly to cats. Unfortunately, cats like how it tastes. Other dangerous products include soaps and medicines.

- Kittens can swallow **small objects** that are left lying around. Keep coins, thumbtacks, paper clips, and other small objects from cats.

- Some **plants** are poisonous to cats. These include ivy, lilies, poinsettias, carnations, and mistletoe. You can get a complete list from a poison-control center.

- Do not leave **windows** open— your cat might jump or fall out.

- Do not leave the **washer and dryer** open. Cats might climb inside. You don't want to accidentally launder your cat!

- Cats might chew on **electrical cords.** If they do, they can be burned or shocked. When you leave your cats alone, unplug any cords they might find.

- A cat can swallow **yarn and string,** which may get caught in its throat or stomach. Make sure yarn and string are not left lying around.

- Use a cat carrier when you **travel** with cats. Never leave a cat in a car in warm weather. Cats cannot easily cool off.

- **Tinsel** is tempting to cats, but they eat it and can't digest it. It's best to do without tinsel on the Christmas tree.

- It's fine for cats to play with paper bags. But do not leave **plastic bags** lying around. If a cat crawls inside a plastic bag, the cat may be unable to breathe.

About a week after I got the kittens, I had a party that was a combination birthday party and cat party. We decorated the house in a cat theme. I invited a lot of my friends—Martha, Korine, Sena, Lalu (that's a nickname for Zelalem, an Ethiopian name), and Zara. We're the "Z" Girls—Zoë, Zelalem, and Zara. Aunt Sarah came, too. Stefan stayed for a little while, but he left because it was a "girls' party."

We played "Pin the Tail on the Cat." And everyone brought cat presents, like toys for the kitties and a book about cats. The kitties liked playing with the wrapping paper as much as the toys! They got pretty wild with all the excitement.

My friends like cats, too. They were all excited to come to a "cat party."

The best part of the party was the cake—in the shape of a cat. Plus, everyone got to play with the kittens.

Of course, my friends wanted to know what the kittens' names were.

"I don't know yet," I said. I was kind of embarrassed.

Everyone had a suggestion for a name.

"I like the name Princess," Martha said.

My brother suggested "Elvis" for the male kitten. Zara said she liked the name Tony.

"Tony?" I asked her. It didn't sound like a cat's name. "Like Tony the Tiger," she said.

Fluffy, Spot, Socks, Mona Lisa, Lucy, Charlie, Max, Samantha. None of the names seemed to fit.

Cats are creatures of habit...

Cats are easy to feed. I just scoop the food into my cats' bowls.

It didn't take long to get used to taking care of my new pets. I feed them and keep their litter box clean. Playing with them is not a chore, but I try to do it every day.

We give our cats dry food, the kind you get at pet stores. It's labeled "nutritionally complete." That means it has everything in it a cat needs to stay healthy. The most important part of their diet is protein. The kitten food has protein and a lot of vitamins. The cats seem to like it.

At first, we followed the instructions on the bag. I moistened the food with a little warm water to make it easier for them to chew. They started with a tiny amount, about 1/4 cup a day. They didn't even eat all of that. They ate just a little at a time.

One of the books I read said you should say your kitten's name as you're feeding it. Then the cat learns its name. It also associates its name with something good—food. I wanted to do that with my kittens right away. There was just one problem—I still hadn't decided what to call them!

When the cats were about 10 months old, we stopped feeding them kitten food. We fed them food for adult cats instead.

Kitten food must work. The cats started growing really fast!

I feed the cats twice a day, once in the morning, and then again when I come home from school. They eat all their food at once, really fast. Cats are creatures of habit—they like to have set mealtimes. When I feed them, I also fill their water bowl with fresh water.

Sometimes we give them special cat treats that we buy at the grocery store. I know some vets say you shouldn't give cats treats or table scraps. But sometimes it's hard to resist! One of my cats likes muffins, cheese, and yogurt. The other one loves popcorn. Every time I eat popcorn, she puts her paw on my leg and begs. I make her sit up on her hind legs and take the popcorn from my fingers.

I don't give my cats treats very often. They have to eat all their regular food first.

Cleaning the cats' litter box is not my favorite thing to do. But it's not that hard. We buy the kind of litter that clumps together when the cats pee. I use a litter scoop with slots to take out the clumps and the poops. I put them in a plastic bag and take them out to the trash. I do that every day.

Once every two weeks, I'm supposed to dump out all the litter and wash the box. I have to admit this is a drag, and I try to put it off. A few times my mom and I argued because I just didn't feel like doing it. But pretty soon I got used to doing these chores. And you know what? It feels kind of good to take care of my cats.

A litter box is pretty easy to clean. Another great thing about cats is they know by instinct how to use a litter box. They don't have to be housetrained, the way dogs do.

Soon after we got the kittens, they began to explore the whole house. They found spots that we didn't even know about! They sniffed every piece of furniture. They found all the possible perches and hiding spots.

Now they have their favorite spots. They both like to sit in the windowsill in the living room. They sit by the window on the front porch, too.

Cats love to sit in windows and look out, and they love to take naps in the sun.

A Cat Loves...

- A warm place to nap—in the sun, on the sofa, by the fire
- To play—with other cats, with you, with toys
- Eating at the same time you do
- A clean, dry litter box that is easy to get to, but out of the way of a lot of activity
- Nibbling on plants (you can grow grass in a pot for your cats if you don't want them eating your plants)
- Gentle combing or brushing
- Being petted—when the cat feels like it!
- Sleeping (especially in bed with you)

A Cat Hates...

- Being cold
- Getting wet
- Being alone for too long
- Not having regular mealtimes; food that is too hot or too cold; dirty food dishes
- A dirty litter box
- Being held if the cat doesn't want to be held
- Loud noises such as the vacuum cleaner, dogs barking, people yelling, thunderstorms

I soon found out that the key word when it comes to kittens is PLAY. They never get tired of playing. They fight with each other, they run, they jump, they leap. They chase anything that moves, including their own tails.

Then there are the toys we got them. One is a furry mouse with catnip inside. The other is a "Cat Dancer," a long wire with rolls of twisted paper tied to the end. When I wiggle the Cat Dancer around, the cats leap up in the air or spring across the floor to chase the paper—I think they think it's a bug. But their favorite toy is like a fishing pole with some feathers at the end. It moves really fast, and the kitties fly through the air to catch the feathers. Sometimes they leap off the couch to get it. That's hilarious.

My cats love to pounce on paper bags. They also chase foil balls or string. They go crazy when I tie a crinkled-up piece of paper to the end of a long piece of string.

Actually, kittens think almost anything is a toy. One day, we came home and found bright yellow feathers scattered all over the whole house. It looked like Big Bird had exploded! (It was really what was left of our feather duster.)

We used to have three spider plants in a window box above the computer. The cats jumped up and knocked down the box. The plants fell all over the computer! I was worried that my dad would be mad. But Stefan and I cleaned up the computer, and luckily it was fine. When I told Dad what happened, he just laughed.

My cats fight, but they don't hurt each other. They're just having fun.

Dad and the cats had to adjust to each other a little.

The funniest thing happened when my mom and dad had some friends over for a party. The tortoiseshell cat jumped onto the coffee table— right into a bowl of dip! Her paw was totally green. She sat there trying to pretend that nothing had happened. Everyone cracked up.

As I spent more time with my kittens, I noticed more things about them. The tortoiseshell has a funny meow—she squeaks. That gave me the idea to name her Squeak. The orange one, who is sort of shy, I decided to call Mouse. It's funny to have a cat named Mouse! Finally, I knew their names.

CHAPTER 4

It was time for them to go to the vet...

Mom and I had no trouble deciding if we should let our cats go outside. The vet told us that cats that stay indoors live longer than cats that go outside—maybe even twice as long.

Cats love being outdoors—hunting mice and birds, nibbling on grass, and climbing trees. But the outdoors is dangerous. There are cars, dogs, and other cats who might be looking for a fight. Outdoor cats can also catch diseases from other animals. Cats can be just as happy indoors, especially if you play with them a lot so they get enough exercise.

My cats are curious about the outdoors. I don't let them out, though.

My cats groom each other. They also "wash up" after they eat.

If cats are cared for properly, they tend to stay healthy. The vet says if I spend time with my cats every day, I will probably notice if they have anything wrong with them. If they start acting strange, they might be sick.

Cats groom themselves by licking their fur. If you've ever had a cat lick you, you know how rough their tongues are. I love watching my cats wash their faces. First they lick one of their front paws. Then they rub that paw around their head and ears. To wash their "private parts," cats stick one foot up in the air and put it behind their neck. It looks funny.

We started brushing them when they were kittens, so they got used to being groomed.

My brother and I brush the cats, too. We brush them once or twice a week. People with long-haired cats have to comb or brush them every day. Long hair gets tangled and messy.

Brushing your cat can also help keep them from getting too many hair balls. Because cats lick themselves so much, they end up with a lot of hair in their stomachs. Then sometimes they throw up a hair ball—a slimy lump of stuck-together fur.

Brushing is a game for Mouse and Squeak. They like chasing the bristles. Mouse loves being brushed. He purrs and rolls over and rubs up against me. But you can't brush his cheeks or he'll go bonkers.

If you're careful, you won't hurt your cat when you trim its nails. Mom is better at this than I am.

Once in a while, Mom trims the cats' front nails. She cuts just the tip of the claws. The cats don't like this very much. They usually squirm and try to get away.

Sena sometimes brushes her cat's teeth, using a child-sized toothbrush. I can see why she does it. Cats have the worst breath! But we haven't brushed our cats' teeth. When we take them to our vet, she checks their teeth and mouths. A cat's breath smells worse than usual if it has a sore or other problem in its mouth.

We took Mouse and Squeak to the veterinarian a few months after we got them. It was time for them to get more shots. First the vet examined them one at a time. She checked their teeth, gums, eyes, ears, and noses. She listened to their heartbeat, felt their bellies, and weighed them.

Squeak hissed and screeched during her exam, but Mouse was quiet. I think they both were scared.

Signs Your Cat Is Sick

You might not know if your cat is sick. Cats don't usually show pain. Often, a hurting cat will simply go off by itself. But you can learn to watch for signs that your cat is sick.

Watch for changes in your cat's habits or personality. Be alert to even small changes. For example, if your cat is eating less than usual, you should see a veterinarian.

Below is a list of the major signs of illness in cats. If your cat shows any of these signs, take it to a vet.

Behavior changes, such as becoming
    unusually quiet or vicious
Bleeding
Blood in stool (poops)
Blood in urine (pee)
Body shaking or twitching
Choking
Coughing
Difficulty swallowing
Drinking more than usual
Drooling
Eating more than usual
Falling down
Hair loss
Head shaking or tilt
Limping
Licking, scratching, or
    biting skin
    more than usual
Loss of appetite

Loss of balance
Lumps, bumps, or masses
Nosebleeds
Panting
Paralysis (inability to move)
    Runny stools (poops)
    Sneezing more than usual
Stiff, swollen, or twitching face
Stomach swelling
Straining to defecate (poop)
Straining to urinate (pee)
    Throwing up
    Urinating more than usual
    Urinating outside litter box
    Voice change
    Weakness
    Weight gain or loss
    Wheezing
    Yellowish eyes or ears

The next time we visited the vet, the cats were eight months old. It was time for them to be sterilized. Mouse, the male, was neutered. Squeak, the female, was spayed. The operations make sure that a female cat won't get pregnant and a male cat won't be able to make a female pregnant.

We talked about it, and we decided we did not want our cats to have babies. There are already too many cats and kittens who aren't wanted. And unneutered tomcats (males) are not fun to live with. They run around and might howl or fight. Worst of all, they spray urine (pee) on walls or on furniture. That's a way of marking their territory, the way cats do in the wild.

Squeak doesn't like shots. I don't blame her!

It was hard to leave the cats at the vet. I worried about them, a little.

We had to leave Mouse and Squeak at the vet's overnight for their operations. I asked the vet to explain what would happen. She said the first thing she does is give the cat a shot so it goes into a deep sleep. That way it doesn't feel any pain or jump off the operating table. Next she shaves the area around the sex organs. That's so no hair will get into the cut. Then she makes a small cut. She removes the sex organs—the uterus and ovaries from a female cat, or the testicles from a male cat. Finally, the cat is stitched up.

After the surgery, the cat is put into a cage to rest. It takes several hours for the cat to wake up. That's why the cats have to stay overnight.

The next day, Mom picked up the cats. We were supposed to let them rest. They slept a lot the first few days after they came home. They didn't eat very much at first. After about a week, they were playing and running around—back to their normal wild selves.

After the cats came home, Squeak was especially quiet. We tried not to bother her much.

Of course, no animal is perfect...

When a cat rubs up against your leg, it's marking you. That's how the cat knows you're one of the "good guys."

Our kittens are growing up fast. I'm getting to know their habits, and I'm learning why they do the things they do. Cats have their own language, if you pay attention to it.

A major way that cats communicate is through the sense of smell. Cats have special scent glands. These glands are near their jaws, on their rear ends, and in their paws. When these glands are rubbed, they release a scent. (Other cats can smell it, but humans can't.) Every cat's scent is different. So cats mark things as "theirs"—trees, other animals, and furniture—by releasing their scent on them. Cats tell friendly animals or people from enemies by marking them.

If you have a cat, you've probably seen it sniff new people who come into your house. My cats sniff me every time I come home from school. I guess they just have to check me out!

Cats greet each other by sniffing, too. At first I thought it was gross that Mouse and Squeak always smell each other's butts. Then I found out why they do it. When a cat sticks its butt in your face, it's being friendly.

By watching my cats, I've learned a lot about them. I can pretty much tell if they're happy or not. When I pet Squeak, she flops over and purrs. She's telling me she wants me to rub her belly. She also likes it when I scratch behind her ears.

When a cat rolls onto its back, it probably wants to be petted. Squeak loves to have her belly rubbed.

Squeak waves her tail when she sees a bird through the window.

A cat's ears say a lot about how the cat feels. When a cat is interested in a friendly way, its ears point forward. When it's getting ready to attack, its ears are pricked up and pointed slightly backward. Ears flattened back mean the cat is afraid.

You can also watch a cat's tail to tell its mood. When a cat is excited, it waves its tail back and forth very quickly. A quietly raised tail is a cat's way of offering a friendly greeting. It's saying, Okay, you can sniff my butt!

Some people think that cats are mean, because they hiss. But a lot of times when cats seem mean, they are really just afraid. The hiss is meant as a warning to keep away.

Many people don't realize that cats can be trained. They can't be trained to sit or stay or lie down when you tell them to, like dogs. But you can teach cats some things. First you have to understand what *they* want to do. Then it's easier to get them to do what *you* want them to do.

I try to tell what my cats are feeling. They have more expressions than you might think.

The most important rule for teaching cats is to use rewards, never punishment. Cats don't learn when you yell at them or hit them. They just get scared. When our cats do something we like, we pet them and praise them.

I pet Mouse when he's being good. He's good most of the time.

When a cat does something it shouldn't do, you can tell it "no." When my cats jump up on the kitchen table or counter, I say "no." Then I gently set them on the floor and stroke them.

Of course, no animal (or human) is perfect. One time my cats pooped outside their litter box. I stepped in it, and I was barefoot. Gross! My mom made me take a bath. I think the cats were mad because we put them in the basement when we had company. When they poop outside the box, that means they're mad.

Cats aren't usually clumsy. But sometimes they knock things over, either accidentally or on purpose.

We keep the scratching post next to the couch. When the cats start to go for the couch, they see the post and scratch that instead.

Scratching furniture or carpet is a big problem for a lot of cat owners. Mouse started scratching our wood furniture. Both cats scratched the couch. So we bought a scratching post. We rub catnip on it, and the cats use it most of the time.

Declawing

Cats scratch. That's just a fact of life. They scratch to mark their territory and to sharpen their claws. Who knows—maybe they scratch just because it feels good. Your cat may scratch your couch, chairs, carpet, or drapes. But you can train your cat so it won't scratch these things. You will need to have a good scratching post. Trimming your cat's claws also helps.

Some people choose to have their cats declawed instead. Declawing is an operation in which the cat's front claws are removed. Some vets say that it's like removing a person's fingernails. Ouch! Many people believe that declawing cats is cruel. In England, people have tried to make the operation against the law. Many veterinarians there will not declaw a cat.

In the United States, declawing is still common. Many people have cats that have been declawed. They say the cats have not suffered any damage. Declawed cats are as lively and playful as cats with claws.

Declawing is usually done when a cat is four to eight months old. The cat is hospitalized for the surgery. After the operation, its feet are bandaged for one or two days. When the cat comes home, its feet will be tender for a couple weeks.

If a cat is declawed, then it must be kept indoors. Without claws, cats can't defend themselves.

Most people who have cats just laugh about these problems. It's not like they are terrible problems that you can't handle. It helps to have a sense of humor. A few years ago, Sena's family got a really big Christmas tree. They decorated it with tons of ornaments and lights. On Christmas Eve, in the middle of the night, there was a huge crash. Everyone woke up and rushed out to the living room. Mica had knocked over the tree, and the room was a big mess. They still laugh about it.

For me, the good things about cats make up for any problems. Yes, cats can be annoying at times. But you still love them. They are good friends.

It's hard to get mad at your cats. They mostly just want you to love them.

Cats were the right choice...

I've had Mouse and Squeak for almost a year. They are also known as the babies, the kids, the little rascals, the darlings, Squeaky-Poo, and Mousehead! All in all, I think that cats were the right choice of pet for my family and me. They are not too much work, and they are good companions. They've even won over my dad. You should see him work on the computer with one of the cats in his lap! He looks seriously comfortable.

My cats are good company. We spend a lot of time together.

Stefan loves the kitties, too. He especially likes watching them fight together. They do it for play, not like a serious fight. They like to sneak up on each other and attack. After they fight, the winner always goes under one certain chair in the living room. The loser goes under another chair.

Squeak goes under the "winner's chair."

Stefan plays rough with Mouse sometimes—I suppose it's because they're both boys.

Mouse never gets tired of playing. I play with the cats every day.

Before too long, my cats got to know my schedule. They tag along with me, whatever I'm doing. Usually they both sleep with me. They know what time I get up. If I don't get up at the right time, Squeak starts bugging me. She meows and climbs around near my head.

As soon as I get up, I feed them. Then I take a shower, and most days they follow me into the bathroom. Sometimes they bat at the shower curtain or try to peek their heads in. Mouse sits on the toilet seat and watches me brush my teeth.

The cats like to be around us, whatever we're doing.

Every day when I come home from school, the cats greet me by rubbing up against me. They know I will feed them and play with them. They also know that I keep their toys in a drawer in the dining room. They sit under the drawer and meow.

At night, the cats like to be in the same room with all of us. If we're watching TV, the cats sit in our laps. When I do my homework, Mouse jumps on the desk. He tries to sit on my papers.

Last summer we went on vacation for a week. We asked a neighbor to come over and feed the cats and take care of the litter. I didn't want to leave them, but they were fine when we came home.

I've had so much fun getting kittens that Sena wants another kitten. She talked her family into getting a playmate for Mica. When I visit Sena's kitten, I will remember when my cats were little.

I am looking forward to having my cats for a long time. Indoor cats often live 15 to 20 years. By the time Mouse and Squeak are 15, I will be almost 25! I guess my parents will have to keep them when I go to college. But that's not for a long time. I have plenty of time to enjoy my cats.

Mouse and Squeak are good friends.

Glossary

Allergies (*al*-er-jees): conditions in which a person becomes sick, gets a rash, sneezes, or has trouble breathing after coming in contact with something that is not harmful to most people

Catnip: a strong-smelling mint plant. Cats are attracted to catnip. They will eat the dried, crumbled leaves. Or they will roll on them and lick them off their fur.

Distemper (diss-*tem*-pur): a disease that is deadly to cats, dogs, and other animals. Signs of distemper are fever, loss of appetite, and weakness.

Hair balls: clumps of hair that form in the stomach of an animal that licks its fur

Housetrained: trained to live in a house

Instinct (*in*-stinkt): a way of feeling or acting that is natural to an animal, rather than learned

Leukemia (loo-*kee*-mee-uh): a disease that affects blood cells. Signs of leukemia in cats are weight loss, depression, and wounds that won't heal.

Purebred (*pyoor*-bred): having ancestors of the same breed

Rabies (*ray*-beez): a disease that affects the brain and spinal cord and may be deadly. Cats, dogs, other animals, and people can get rabies. It causes choking and makes the muscles tighten and twitch.

Territory (*ter*-uh-tor-ee): an area chosen by an animal as its own

Vaccinations (vak-suh-*nay*-shuns): shots that protect animals (or people) from certain diseases

Resources

Delta Society
289 Perimeter Road East
Renton, WA 98055
(206) 226-7357
An international organization for studying
human-animal relationships. Will send a list of books
on animal topics.

Food and Drug Administration
Center for Veterinary Medicine
7500 Standish Place
Metro Park North 2
Rockville, MD 20855
Will send a free pamphlet on cat care.

Humane Education Department
Humane Society of Denver
2080 S. Quebec Street
Denver, CO 80231
(303) 696-4941
Education department staff will answer questions on
handling behavior problems in dogs and cats.

Humane Society of the U.S.
2100 L Street NW
Washington, DC 20037
(202) 452-1100
Free tips on caring for birds, dogs, cats, and small
mammals.

Tree House Animal Foundation
(312) 784-5488, Wed.–Sun.
(773) 784-5577, Hotline open 7 days a week.
Specializes in behavior questions. Caller pays long-
distance charges, but consultation is free.

For Further Reading

Alderton, David. *Cats.* (Eyewitness Handbooks.) New York: Dorling Kindersley, 1992.

Arnold, Caroline. *Cats: In from the Wild.* Minneapolis: Carolrhoda, 1993.

Cole, Joanna. *A Cat's Body.* New York: William Morrow, 1982.

George, Jean Craighead. *How to Talk to Your Cat.* New York: Warner Books, 1985.

Jankowski, Connie. *Adopting Cats and Kittens.* New York: Howell Book House, 1993.

Müller, Ulrike. *The New Cat Handbook.* Woodbury, NY: Childrens Press Choice/Barron's, 1984.

Overbeck, Cynthia. *Cats.* Minneapolis: Lerner, 1983.

Piers, Helen. *Taking Care of Your Cat.* Hauppauge, NY: Barron's, 1992.

The Reader's Digest Illustrated Book of Cats. Montreal: The Reader's Digest Assn. (Canada), 1992.

Walls, Jerry G. *Kittens as a New Pet.* Neptune City, NJ: T.F.H. Publications, 1991.

Index

ABOUT THE AUTHOR

LeeAnne Engfer is a writer and editor. She graduated from the University of Minnesota with degrees in journalism and French. Her interests include animals, books, cooking, travel, and yoga. She lives in St. Paul, Minnesota, with three cats.

ABOUT THE PHOTOGRAPHER

Andy King is a native of Boulder, Colorado, and a graduate of Colorado State University. Andy has traveled around the world as a documentary and corporate photographer, and he has worked as a photographer at newspapers in Minnesota and Texas. He lives with his wife, Patricia, and their daughter in St. Paul, Minnesota, where he enjoys mountain biking and playing basketball.